Contents

Magician

Leila is pretending to
be a magician.
She has made a pink
rabbit appear in
her top hat.

Let's pretend we a

Entertainers

Karen Bryant-Mole

Heinemann
LIBRARY

First published in Great Britain by Heinemann Library, Halley Court, Jordan Hill, Oxford OX2 8EJ, a division of Reed Educational & Professional Publishing Ltd.

OXFORD FLORENCE PRAGUE MADRID ATHENS MELBOURNE AUCKLAND KUALA LUMPUR
SINGAPORE TOKYO IBADAN NAIROBI KAMPALA JOHANNESBURG GABORONE
PORTSMOUTH NH (USA) CHICAGO MEXICO CITY SAO PAULO

Designed by Jean Wheeler

Commissioned photography by Zul Mukhida

Produced by Colourpath Ltd., Soho.

Printed and bound in Italy by L.E.G.O.

02 01 00 99 98
10 9 8 7 6 5 4 3 2 1

ISBN 0 431 04651 4

This title is also available in a hardback library edition (ISBN 0 431 04650 6).

British Library Cataloguing in Publication Data
Bryant-Mole, Karen
Let's pretend we are entertainers
1.Entertainers - Juvenile literature
2.Readers (Primary)
I.Title II.Entertainers
790

Words that appear in the text **in bold** can be found in the glossary.

Acknowledgements
The Publishers would like to thank the following for permission to reproduce photographs. Cephas; 5 Stuart Boreham, 15 Nicholas James, Chapel Studios; 7 Tim Garrod, 11 and 23 Graham Horner, 13 Tim Richardson, Eye Ubiquitous; 19 Mike Southern, Tony Stone Images; 9 Geoff Johnson, 21, Zefa; 17.

Every effort has been made to contact copyright holders of any material reproduced in this book. Any omissions will be rectified in subsequent printings if notice is given to the Publisher.

Magicians often use a magic wand when
they make things appear and disappear.
This magician can do card tricks, too.

Pop singer

Bartie enjoys pretending to be a pop singer. He is using a hairbrush as a microphone.

This singer is singing into a real microphone.
The microphone makes the singer's voice
sound louder.

Acrobat

Gemma is pretending to be an acrobat. She is trying to balance a plastic cup on her head!

Acrobats have to be very good at balancing. This acrobat is balancing on a special cycle called a **unicycle**.

Band player

Aliyu is marching
as he plays his
toy drum.
He is pretending
to be a band player.

These band players can march, read the music and play their **instruments** all at the same time. They have their music in special holders on their sleeves.

Film actor

Melissa would like to be a film star.
She is dressed up as an explorer.
Megan is pretending to film her.

These actors are dressed
in **old-fashioned** clothes.
The man in front of the camera tells
everyone that filming is about to start.

Puppeteer

Bartie is making his
puppet walk along
the floor.
This type of puppet is
called a **string puppet**.

These puppets are called **glove puppets**.
The person who is working the puppets is
hidden inside the striped tent.

Ballet dancer

Gemma wears a **tutu** when she pretends to be a ballet dancer. She is practising pointing her toes.

Real ballet dancers have to practise
for many hours every day.
It takes a lot of work to become as
good as these dancers.

Juggler

Leila is learning how to juggle.
She starts by learning how to
juggle with just two balls.

Some jugglers can juggle with any objects
they are given.
These men are using special juggling clubs.

Clown

Aliyu has dressed up as a clown. He is wearing a bright green wig and a big red nose.

Clowns make people laugh.
They wear funny clothes and do
funny things.

Conductor

Megan is listening to some music and pretending to be a conductor.
She is using a plastic spoon as a conductor's **baton**.

Conductors stand in front of the **orchestra**.
They use a baton to make sure that everyone
plays the music at the same speed.

Glossary

baton a special stick used by a conductor

glove puppet a puppet worked by putting your hand inside it

instruments objects that people can make music with

old-fashioned from a long time ago

orchestra a group of people who play musical instruments together

string puppet a puppet worked by strings attached to pieces of wood

tutu a ballet costume with a net skirt

unicycle a cycle with only one wheel

Index